BETWEEN YOU VOLUME 2

FATEMA KAPADIA

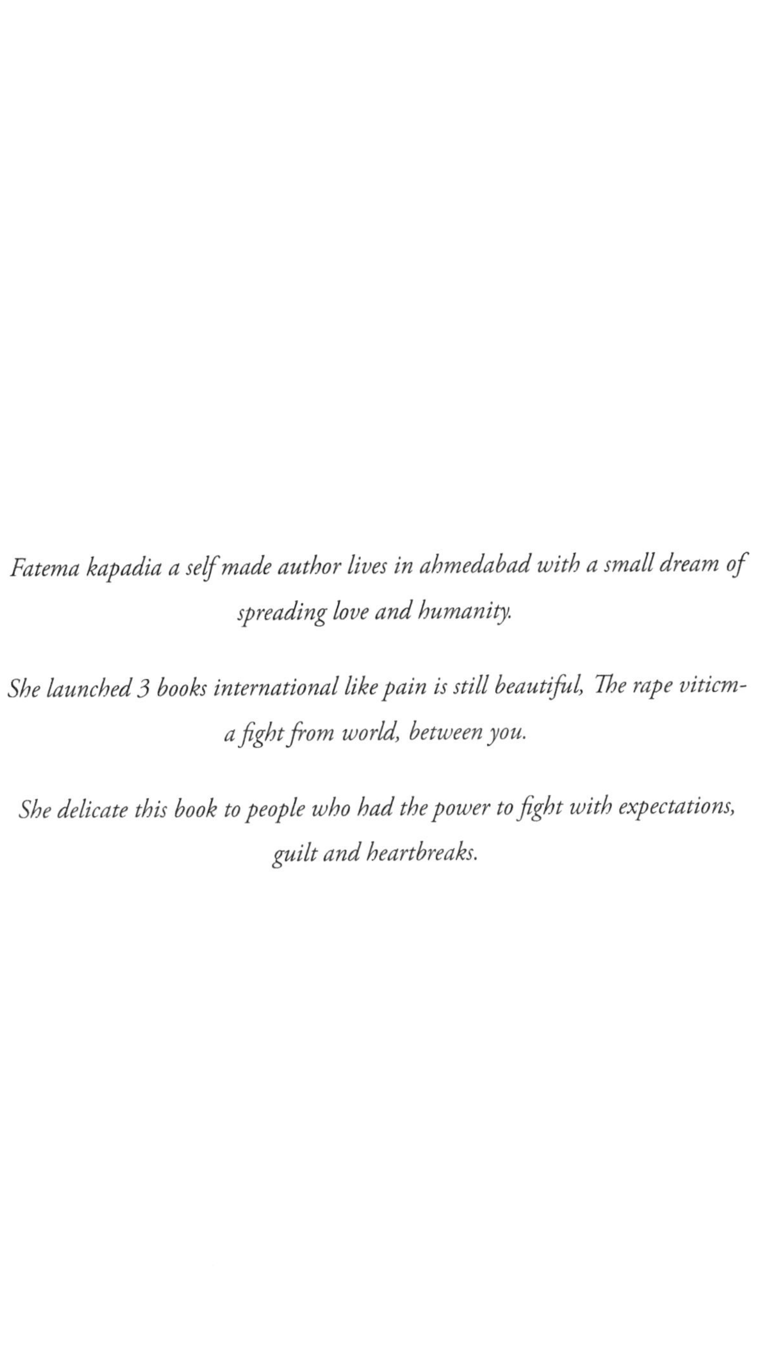

Fatema kapadia a self made author lives in ahmedabad with a small dream of spreading love and humanity.

She launched 3 books international like pain is still beautiful, The rape viticm-a fight from world, between you.

She delicate this book to people who had the power to fight with expectations, guilt and heartbreaks.

Contents

Contents

Foreword

Expectations, Guilt, heartbreaks ?

    Oh darling dealing all this alone?

    Take a breath.

    Have a look.

    See what this all gives you.

Prologue

- *Phase 1: - Expectations.*
- *phase 2:- Guilt.*
- *phase 3 :- Heartbreak.*

1. Phase 1: - Expectations.

**Sometimes
we create
our own
heartbreaks
through
expectation.**

Expecting more getting less

When you expect more from peoples, place , things etc you get attached more.

Whether they are your friends , your family, your love , or anyone in life they get changed and this change is going on by time to time.

And one fine day that all thing you expected from them it will break you.

The more you expect the less you get .

The more you run the more far they go.

The more you try to chase the more you loose.

This is life darling you are on someone and someone is on you.

In life where every thing is temporary why this feelings have permanent place in this world.

Whether it love , sacrifices, hate, happy , sad , live laugh goes so deep in our heart ?

Ever ask this question why?

Because when you do anything from about you do it for your self.

If you love you love for your heart.

If you sacrifice you sacrifice for your loved ones.

You hate because your heart hate that.

You live , laugh , became sad it's all because you have all for this in you.

Not everyone deserves your all emotions.

So stop running for people .

When you try to win someone's heart you do every thing.

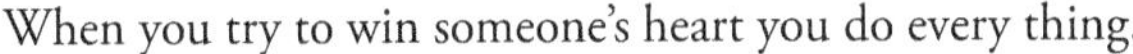

You do is laugh for them

You do is wait for them .

You do is cry for them .

You do is overthink for them.

But at the end your expectations from them increase to high and they just leave you without even telling you.

So expect less live more.

Live on time .

May be this time teach you about things.

May be this time teach you to wait.

May be this time teach you to survive.

May be this time teach you to heal.

And may be to expect less from people.

Ever notice that the person you are expecting anything from them and they never did anything for you.

The same way other person who is expecting the things from you and you never did.

Relatable?

When people set a level for you or you set a level for people you expect accordingly.

Sometimes you fail and sometimes they fail.

But between Expectations and failures we break .

We break because we expect the things to go accordingly.

Sometimes it's good if things don't work.

Sometimes it's good if you break .

Sometime it good set and thing about what didn't go accordingly.

And in this sometime you live Expecting less

Expectations for your own people.

Its not possible that you don't expect for your loved one's.

We human expect automatically.

It's not possible for us to don't expect for our families, from our best friends, from our relationship etc.

We expect the things.

And this automatically Expectations hurt us more .

When this Expectations break we break too.

We lost everything.

The journey of Expectation smile to the journey of expectation cry is most difficult.

"The journey was difficult

I didn't expected to end this but ended why?

"

Expected good .

But ended bad.

It's ok atleast you tried hard .

Atleast you can console your heart by saying I thought of but didn't work out .

Like we expect this from our people this people's also expect things from us.

The game of expectation can't be one side it has to be on both side.

Positivity and negativity both are effect of this expectations.

The only thing matters is priority.

Expectations from ourselves.

Most things are hurt by our own self.

We expect everything from ourselves.

Mostly good .

But we forget at the end we are humans only.

Sometime it's only who made you cry , heart breaks and disappoint.

2. Phase 2 :- Guilt

Guilt of not saying.

Sometime you wait for right time .

Sometimes you wait for right person to share .

Sometimes you wait for other to say first .

And at the end you do is just wait.

You feel guilt about not saying the things at right time.

So stop feeling that guilt.

Maybe you wait for right time but you didn't have to feel that guilt .

Its oki if the things didn't work out at time .

Maybe it was not right time to speak .

Maybe that time you had to be silent.

Maybe you were right .

And this maybe is your life.

So stop to feel guilt.

Guilt of not sharing to right person.

Your feelings are ocean.

Your heart is lake.

Your mind is river.

Your soul is pure.

After a person leaves you forever you always find things to share with .

You always think of maybe I must have told them about everything.

No man you are wrong there is no right person to share.

Telling everything to that right person maybe console you mind and heart .

But stop being guilty about not able to share the things with right person.

People leave.

Place break,

But life continues.

Note:- Maybe to many I must be sounding selfish or self obsessed but the guilt you our putting on your self is more hard.

Be gentle to your self.

People leave ,

Time don't wait.

Something like that happened?

Many of you must.

But darling everything thing is planned by destiny.

You wait for others to be first but this other leave you forever.

You feel maybe I must have told them first and this maybe feel you guilty of
not telling

So why you feel guilt on it ?

And this is for them

You thought of holding

You thought of sharing,

You thought of peace.

But destiny might work for you.

You thought of them

And they thought of other.

Its oki my love,

Maybe its someone else to share.

Its oki if plan didn't work out.

But at the end you do is feel guilt for not telling first.

Why so ?

Don't feel guilty of not saying

Don't feel guilty of not holding

Don't feel guilty of not sharing.

Its oki.

You are sea that never stop

When people leave you break badly.

You stop trusting process.

You stop cycle of life

You fear of new chapter of life.

You fear of doing things again.

You fear of loosing yourself once again.

And you do is just wait.

But after some years you feel guilty of wasting time on that .

But you don't need to feel guilt on it this years have teach you many things.

When your life cycle stop ,

When you can't find the way .

When your are stuck on roads of darkness

This time to your self helps you.

So stop feelings guilty.

Nothing is bad.

Nothing can stop you.

Trust the process.

Note:- Everything happens for reason.

What you are today you will not be that tomorrow.

Time is best teacher.

Guilt of hope

Hope the light of life.

We always hope things that matters us

Despite we dont know whether this hope is other ones bad thing.

Peace on souls of hope that end there hopes.

When people leave the hope on something they become hard like rock.

And rock is of guilt that broke the hope .

You choose to lose hope ,

You choose to give up,

You choose to never fight that again,

You choose to set again ,

You choose to leave .

Sometimes it's better to leave .

Sometimes Its better to lose the to gain.

Sometimes it's better to stop fighting.

Sometimes its batter to stay came.

Don't feel guilty of not fighting back .

Don't feel guilty if you leave all your Hope's.

Don't feel guilty of not trying once more.

Don't feel guilty if you are tried of hoping .

After all you too need rest.

It's not important to always hope to score good.

Sometimes you can stay clam.

Be gentle on yourself.

People will always demand,

People will always compare you.

So let's stop this guilt of hope.

Guilt of your mistakes.

Remember one think you are not by your mistakes.

Mistakes are natural man made thing that happens.

Unknowingly you hurt someone is a unknown mistake you did.

But the mistakes doesn't define you.

Problems and mistakes are part of life .

What ever happens for something which will come in future.

In life where every one is dealing with some or other thing this mistake help you find right part.

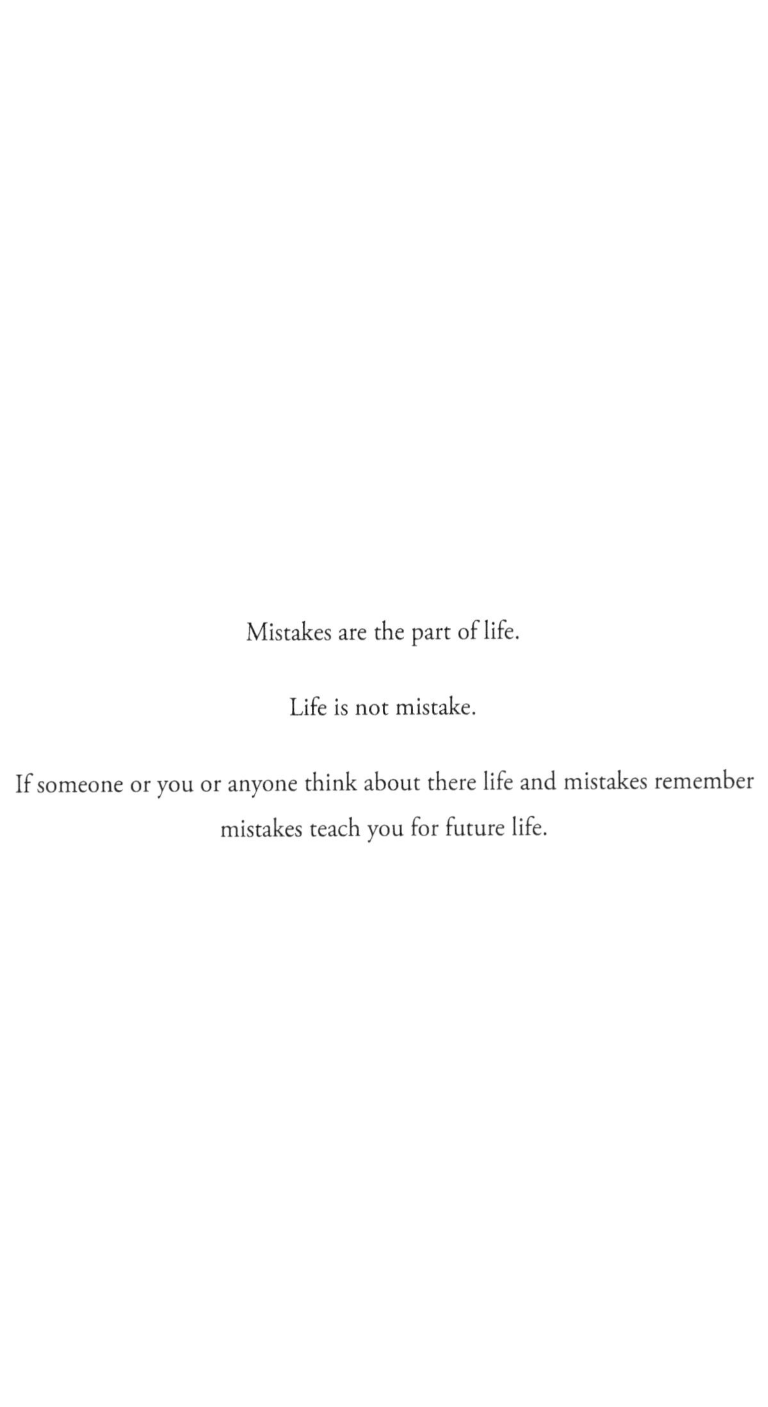

Mistakes are the part of life.

Life is not mistake.

If someone or you or anyone think about there life and mistakes remember mistakes teach you for future life.

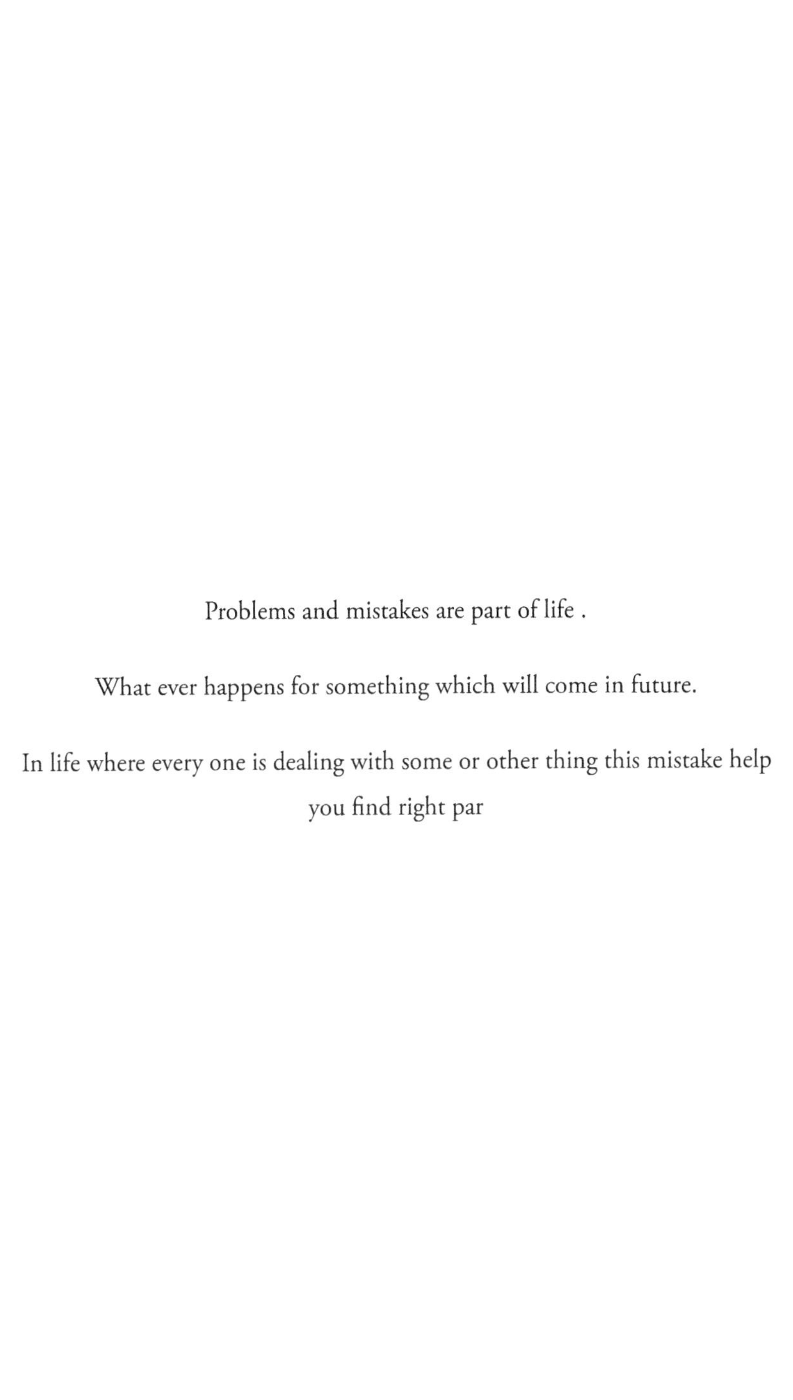

Problems and mistakes are part of life .

What ever happens for something which will come in future.

In life where every one is dealing with some or other thing this mistake help you find right par

Guilt of leave every one behind.

When you leave every one behind some part of you also leave with them.

Good one bad one.

Sometimes you value that human the most rather there behaviour.

Leaving every one on every time is part of life .

Guilt of not choosing your happiness.

When we are too good by heart we are only one how sacrifice ourselves happiness.

Every time you choose others first rather you own.

You sacrifice your dream , your people, your thoughts, your emotions, your love , your peace, your every thing.

Guilt of cheat..

When the chapter of cheat comes we all fell our conscience.

Now that you know some how I became stable .

Now that the part of me had cheated you I can't help to face anything.

You or me both were on the same paper but mine had the drop of black

3. Phase 3 :-   Depression.

Enter Caption

<u>Trauma of not saying</u>

When the matter of not saying comes in front .

We became the most terrible person on earth.

We suffer from inner confusion of saying , sharing and confessing .

We feel devastated.

We don't find ourselves out of saying and confessing our own feelings.

The truth with depression is we want to talk but we can't and just do is ignore.

We do is cry in alone. We do is cry in alone. We do is cry in alone.

We do is cry in alone.

As of now your therapy is crying.

You cry on small thing that dont ever matter to you.

You do is cry on that lonely nights and feel more anxious.

You can't even think about yourself is devastating.

You feel all alone all the time .

Note :- *when you try to not cry you hold many scare .*

Cry but once you stop crying dont allow your self to remember again that reason of cry .

This will help you to come our of depression slowly and steadily.

To who so ever

If you thing you or your loved once is going to this trauma please remember deal softly with them.

Because a person may look cool and cherish but deep insides they are hurt .

The most common thing in desperation is seen is they dont show things .

But when they are alone the cry like the heal .

So deal softly with them .

Whether teenagers or younger there loved ones should look out there odd behavior and remember to deal softly and steady with them.

<u>Fear of loosing other things.</u>

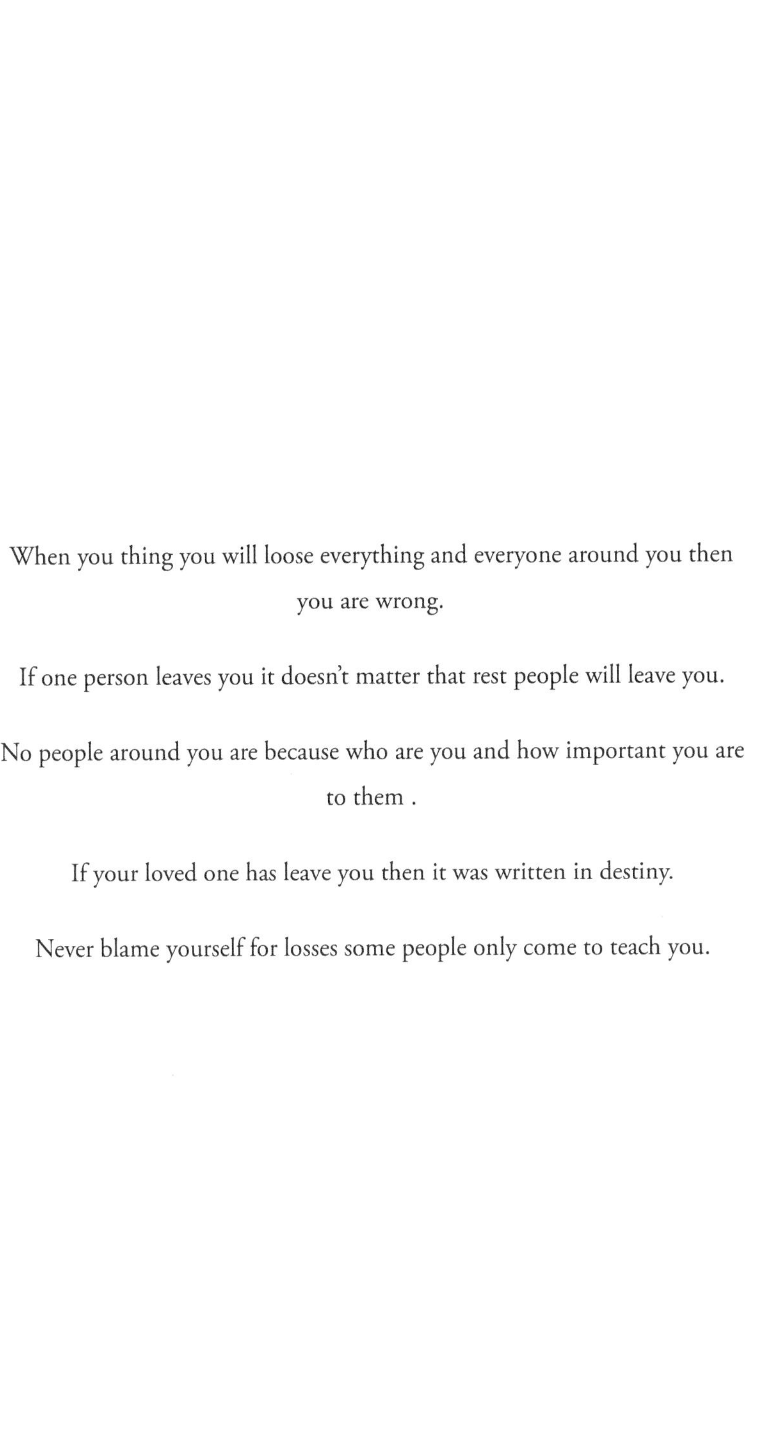

When you thing you will loose everything and everyone around you then you are wrong.

If one person leaves you it doesn't matter that rest people will leave you.

No people around you are because who are you and how important you are to them .

If your loved one has leave you then it was written in destiny.

Never blame yourself for losses some people only come to teach you.

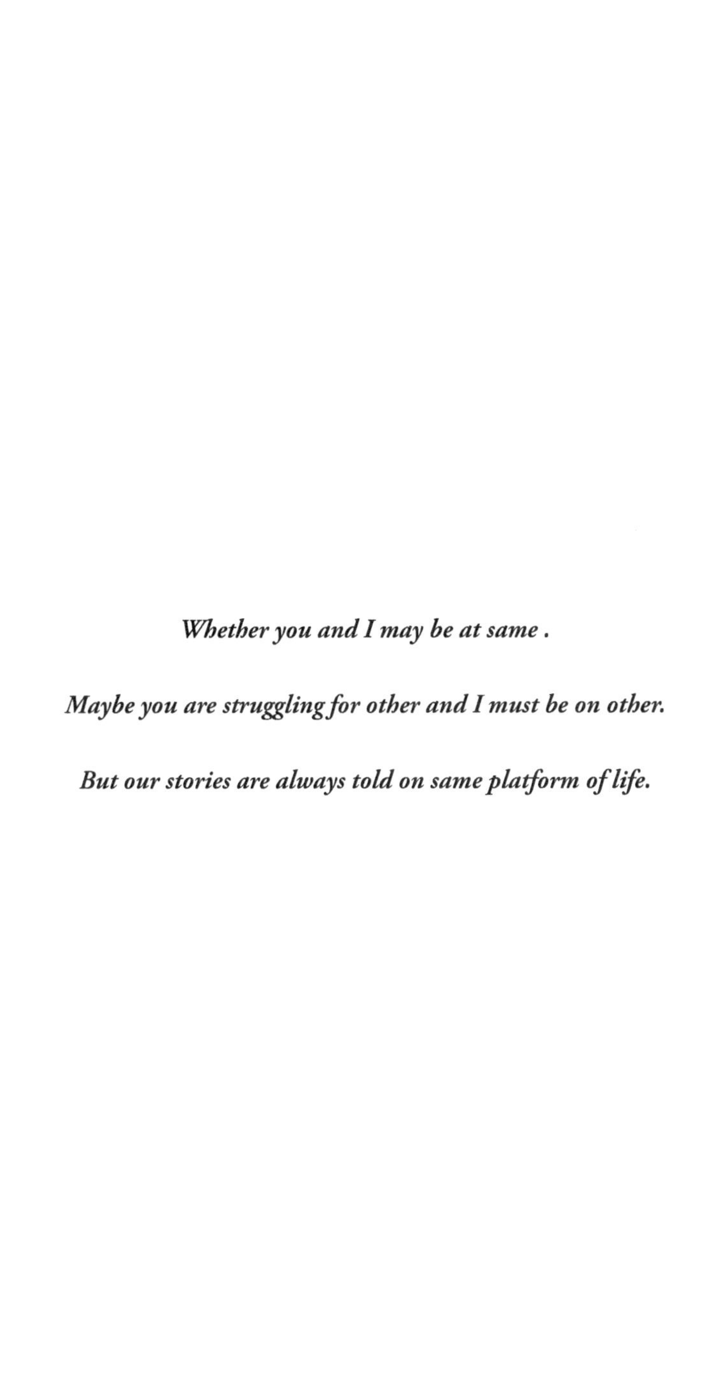

Whether you and I may be at same .

Maybe you are struggling for other and I must be on other.

But our stories are always told on same platform of life.

Note :- <u>when you loose the unthought person you become the most hurt person.</u>

<u>Some are not meant to be there forever.</u>

<u>Some chapter can get over.</u>

<u>And maybe that chapter can't come till the end.</u>

<u>So that doesn't matter your book is over that means that part is over book goes on .</u>

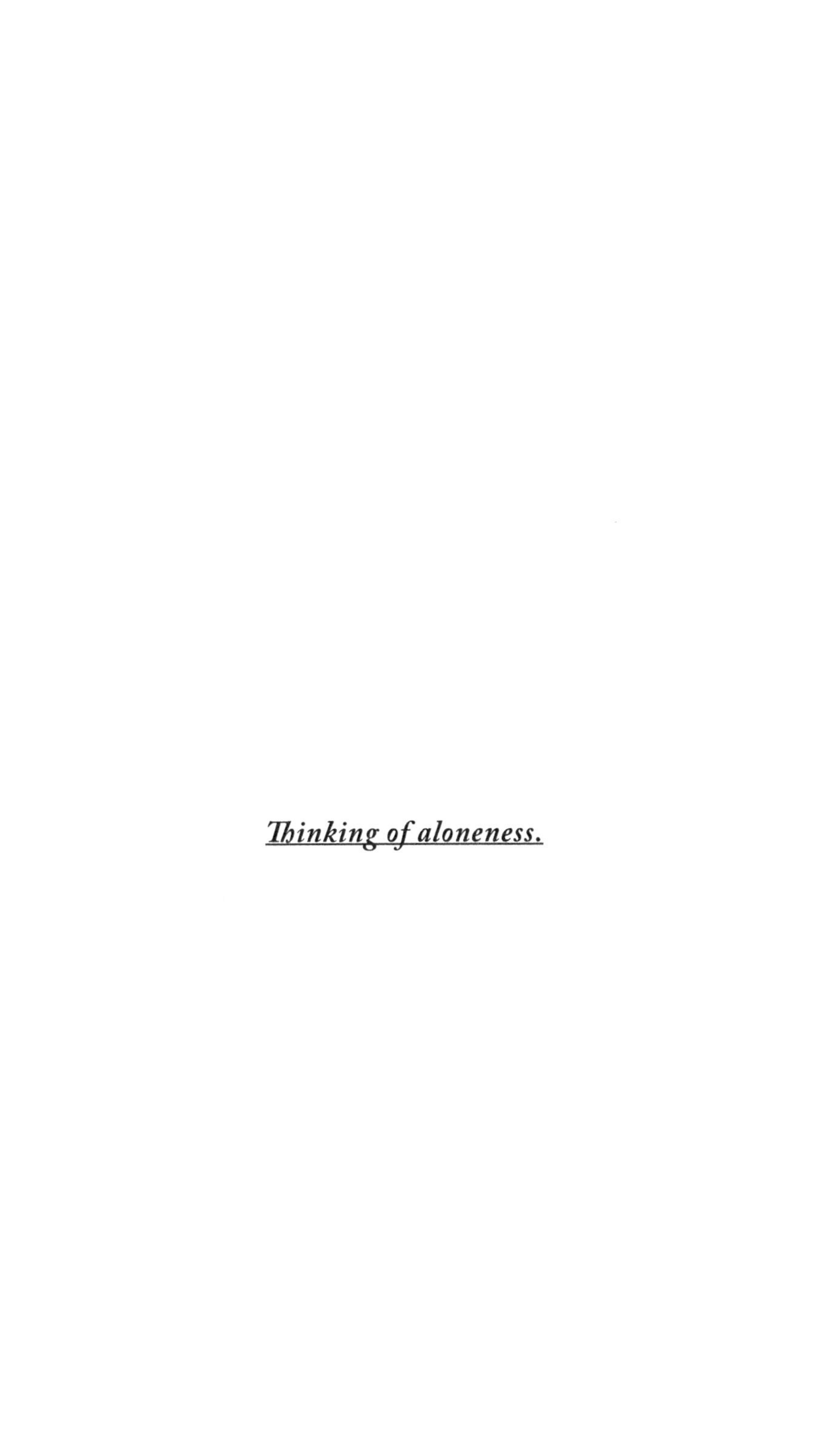
Thinking of aloneness.

Aloneness is part of you.

You have be do some part of your life alone .

In that part no one is with you.

You have to deal with all thing alone.

When most trusted persons replace you . You go though many breakdowns.

Your pain is unbearable.

Your trust is broken and you thing you can't trust any one again.

Your heart had got the big hole .

Your brain system had stop to work.

Your anger reach to the top of cloud.

You thing of not trusting people again .

<u>Agree???</u>

Note To self

Note :- <u>But you have to remember one thing its oki maybe this was a good lesson.</u>

<u>There is a quote</u>

<u>"Good things gives you memories</u>

<u>Worst things gives you lesson ."</u>

<u>Decided what you got .</u>

Some times we all need a shoulder to cry .

Remember depression is not only a phase of life.

It is the most tough part of life.

The last stage of depression is like cancer that slowly kill you from inside .

Your soul and mind both are done with each other.

And at the end you all want is peace for your self.

But remeber you are fighter and at the end of the race you have to win.

win from this cancer and in future this cancer will help you to become succesful.